D1434853

BUILDINGS

David Cook

HarperCollins*Publishers*

First published in 1993
by HarperCollins Publishers
London

© Diagram Visual Information 1993

Editors: Louise Clairmonte, Margaret Doyle, John Morton
Art Director: Darren Bennett
Contributing artists: James Dallas,
Roger Hutchins, Lee Lawrence, Ali Marshall,
Philip Patenall, Bruce Robertson, Graham Rosewarne

All rights reserved. No part of this publication may be reproduced,
stored in a retrieval system, or transmitted, in any form or by any
means, electronic, mechanical, photocopying, recording or otherwise,
without the prior written permission of the publishers.

A catalogue record for this book is available from the British Library

ISBN 0 00 412670 X

Printed and bound in Hong Kong

CONTENTS

Tools and Equipment

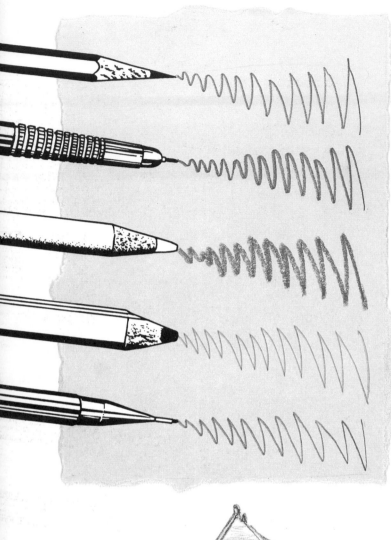

Pencils

Pencil is one of the most versatile drawing media available. It can be used for final, detailed drawings as well as for quick, rough sketches.

Pencils are graded by hardness, from 9H, the hardest, through H, B and up to 9B, the softest. Harder pencils make fainter, sharper lines; softer ones make heavier, rough-edged lines.

Many different types of pencil are available: clutch, propelling, wax and coloured, and special ones designed for engineers, carpenters and printers.

Erasing is easy, and you can create special effects by rubbing out some areas or smudging with your finger. Be sure to spray your final drawing with a fixative to make it permanent.

Try different grades and types of pencils to become familiar with the different effects each produces.

For this drawing of a priory, the artist used a B pencil on tracing paper

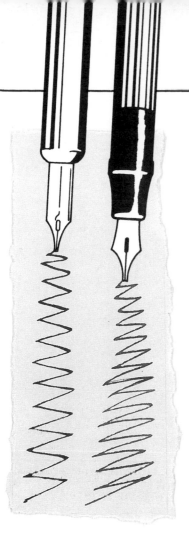

This row of cottages was drawn using a technical pen on smooth paper

Pens

Choosing a pen can be difficult. There are many types, each with a distinct quality.

Fountain and **dip pens** come with nibs of different widths which make lively lines of varying thickness.
Felt-tip pens also come in several thicknesses. They can create bold drawings in vibrant colours. Some have tips like paintbrushes.
Technical pens make accurate, even lines and are best for careful, detailed work.

Protect felt-tip pens or markers by replacing their caps. Don't damage technical or dip pens with too much pressure. Ink pens or brushes are easily cleaned after use, but ink left too long will clog, making smooth lines hard to draw – always wash out ink after sketching trips!

Remember that pen marks are final; they cannot be erased. Sometimes it helps to make a pencil sketch first, adjusting it as you like, and then you can go over your final lines in pen.

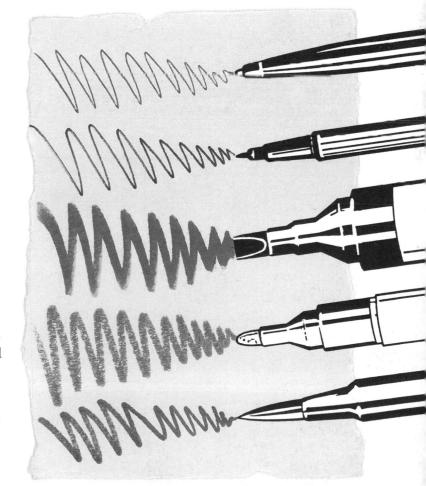

The rough texture and shadows in the sketch of the Vila Viçosa, Portugal (*above*), are emphasized using conté crayon on rough paper

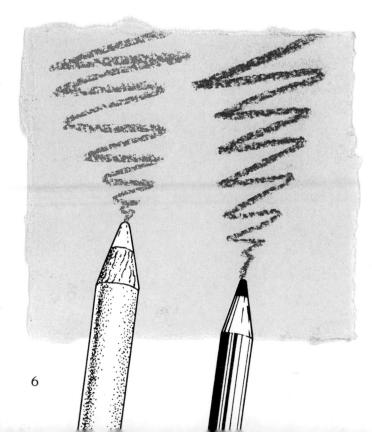

Pastels, crayons and charcoal

You will find that pastels, crayons and charcoal are very different from other drawing tools. They make a wide variety of tones and lines, have a lively, textured feel, and inspire spontaneity in your drawings.

Soft, oil-based **pastels** come in a wide range of vibrant colours. The colour will be strong whether you use a single stroke or go over your drawing many times, giving the appearance of an oil painting.

Wax **crayons**, like pastels, also let you pick from a spectrum of colours. Both pastels and crayons are difficult to draw fine detail with, but they give a fresh, textured look and combine well with other media.

Like pen marks, pastel and crayon lines are hard to rub out. You might want to draw a pencil sketch, then go over the lines in pastel or crayon for your final drawing.

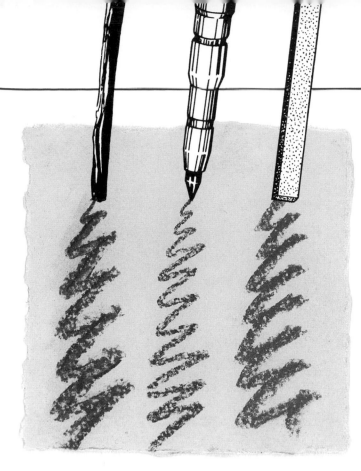

Charcoal gives a bold effect. A soft, crumbly stick, it can smudge easily. After some practice, however, you'll find that it can also be used for quite detailed drawings.

Conté crayon, in stick form like charcoal, doesn't smudge or break as easily. You can use the side of the stick as well as the tip.

Protect your drawing, as you work, by keeping a clean piece of paper under your hand as you rest it on the paper, and by spraying your final work with a fixative.

You can smudge on purpose, to create a special effect, by rubbing with your finger or a piece of kneaded dough over selected areas. Rubbing out can also create white areas that act as highlights in your drawing.

The sketch below, of a tiny chapel at Mugginton, in Derbyshire, was made using charcoal on cartridge paper, which gave high contrast. Varied pressure helped to create different textures

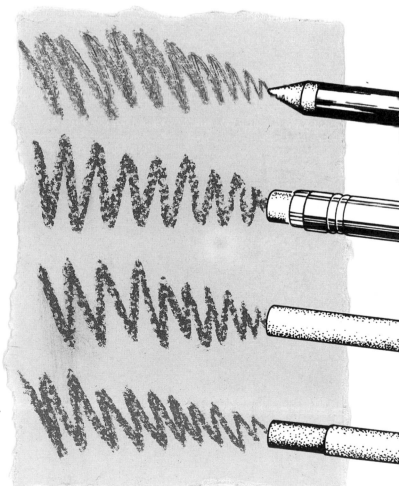

Brushes

When used carefully, and with practice, brushes can create both bold, energetic images and finely detailed paintings.

You can choose from a variety of thicknesses and lengths, each suitable for a particular purpose. **Short-tipped, pointed** brushes are for fine detail. **Long-tipped, pointed** brushes can create both thick and thin lines.
Flat brushes, both short and long tipped, are best for filling in larger areas of your drawing.
Oriental brushes are versatile, making lines of variable thickness.

Brushes also vary in the quality and type of fibre used. Synthetic brushes, the least expensive, are suitable for many purposes. Best results can be achieved using a pure sable brush. This type is expensive, but can last for years.

Care for your brushes by not overloading them with paint, handling them gently (so as not to damage the 'spring' of the bristles), cleaning them after each time they are used and storing them upright.

Wet media

Many paints and inks are water based, so you can dilute them to get different strengths of colour. Watercolours, for example, can be bright or muted, and they create soft effects, especially when used on soft, thick paper.

With wet media you will need to work on a heavy type of paper. You will also need a palette on which to mix your paints, and a surface on which to place your jars of ink, paint and water and your extra brushes.

Wax or pastel crayons can be used with water-based paints: as the two won't mix, special effects can be created. Using both wet and dry media in this way may enhance your artwork.

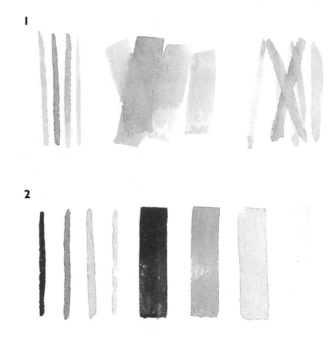

I

2

I These watercolour brush strokes give different results on the same paper; they were made with (*from left to right*) a small, pointed tip; a flat brush; a large, pointed tip

2 Water is used to vary watercolour tones, greater quantities of water producing lighter tones. These different strokes show how tone changes with the amount of water used

3

4

3 When laying a solid area of watercolour, try to maintain an even tone. Beginning with a light tone, gradually increase tone by adding darker tones to the wet wash underlay

4 Letting an area of watercolour dry before you brush more paint on top of it prevents the new layer of paint from blending and will produce distinct changes in tone and colour

Strong, bold lines, made with watercolour brushes on watercolour paper, produced this painting of a favourite pub (*right*)

5

5 Using a little water to dampen your paper surface will make watercolour spread and diffuse into the paper. This produces soft and delicate edges around your brush strokes

6

6 Brushing ink or dark, more concentrated watercolour onto dampened paper can produce striking and unusual effects

Newsprint is inexpensive making it good for sketching and practising

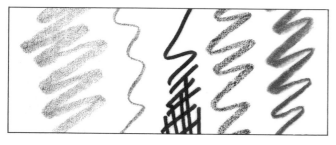

Tracing paper is semi-transparent so it lets you trace other images quickly

Stationery paper is usually available in one standard size. It works well with pen

Cartridge paper, usually textured and of a high quality, is one of the most versatile surfaces

Surfaces to draw on

Like drawing tools, surfaces have their own character.

When choosing a surface, consider the type of medium – pencil, brush, watercolour, pastel – and the overall effect you want to obtain – soft tones, sharp detail, rich colour, and so on.

Some surfaces are better with certain drawing tools than others. Pencil can be used on papers, but not on plastic or glass. Paints, especially watercolours, are best on thick, heavy papers.

These are guidelines, not hard-and-fast rules. Don't be afraid to try different drawing tools on different papers. By experimenting, you will discover the combinations that you are most comfortable with and that give you the results you want.

Paper is made in one of three ways.
Handmade paper, although expensive, is of the best quality and is long-lasting. Being handmade, each sheet is somewhat different.
Mould paper is formed sheet-by-sheet, like handmade paper, but by a machine. It has a wrong and a right side.
Machine-made paper is of a uniform quality – that is, each sheet is the same. It is produced in a continuous roll and cut into sheets later.

The texture of the paper is determined by special treatments. A paper or board that is hot-pressed is smooth; one that is not has a slightly rough texture. Wove and laid papers have a subtle, continuous texture that reflects the pattern of the mould used to form the sheet.

The strokes shown on the left and right of these pages indicate (*from left to right*) the effect of a 3B pencil, a 2B pencil, a felt-tip pen, a conté crayon and a piece of charcoal on different types of drawing surfaces.

The strong drawing of a church tower (*opposite*) was made using felt-tip pens on smooth paper

Ingres paper is often used with charcoal or pastels. It is available in white and pale shades

Watercolour paper is thick and absorbent, so it works well with wet media

Bristol board is stiff, with a smooth surface, and is best for pen drawings

Layout paper is a semi-opaque, lightweight paper that works best with pencils and pens

Choosing the Right Medium

1

2

3

The drawings on these pages are all of the same half-timbered cottages by a river – yet each is quite different. This is because the different media and techniques used give each of them a unique appearance. Tools and surfaces combine to determine the 'feel' of your final drawing. Pastels and watercolours, for instance, create softer, more blended images, especially when used on soft, absorbent papers. Hard pencils and pens used on tracing paper or smooth board allow more detail and sharper lines, giving the drawing a more precise feel.

The tool you use also affects your technique – the type of marks you make when drawing. Some tools allow you to make many different types of marks. With a pencil, for example, you can make short sketchy lines or you can blend lines together for a softer feel. Dip pens are excellent for sharp, precise lines, as in technical drawings, or for making patterns to create textures.

Drawing tools and surfaces are discussed in more detail on pp. 4–11.

Try to become familiar with a variety of drawing tools and paper surfaces; if you are uncomfortable with your equipment, it will show in your final drawing. Learn which tools and surfaces produce which effects, and before starting your drawing, decide which to use by considering the appearance you want to create.

The drawings on these pages were made with the following combinations of tools and surfaces:

1 Soft pencil on cartridge paper
2 Dip pen on cartridge paper
3 Charcoal on Ingres paper
4 Ball-point pen on Bristol board
5 Watercolour on watercolour paper
6 Coloured pencil on cartridge paper
7 Hard pencil (HB) on tracing paper
8 Pastels on Ingres paper
9 Felt-tip pen on layout paper

4

7

5

8

6

9

Measuring in Drawing

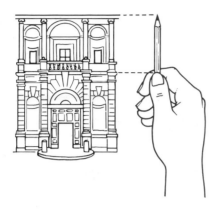

Pencil measuring
Hold your pencil upright in your outstretched hand (*left*), with the thumb uppermost on the pencil. Lining up the top of the pencil with the top of the object you want to measure, use your thumb to mark the bottom of the object. Keeping your thumb in place, move the pencil to the paper to transfer the measurement.

Transferring what you see accurately onto paper is one of the most difficult drawing tasks. There are several simple ways to make this task easier.

Be careful not to misjudge the size of objects in the distance. Check your accuracy by measuring the object. You can do this easily from where you stand by using your hand, a ruler, or your pencil.

To begin drawing the entrance opposite, I first drew a grid with a horizontal line at eye-level and a central vertical line (*below left*). I measured the entrance's proportions with a pencil. Working in sequence, I began to outline the main elements in relation to the grid

As I was working with a soft 2B pencil, the original vertical and horizontal grid lines soon began to disappear into the background as I sketched in the lines that would represent the roof, storeys, columns, windows and recesses of the entrance (*below*)

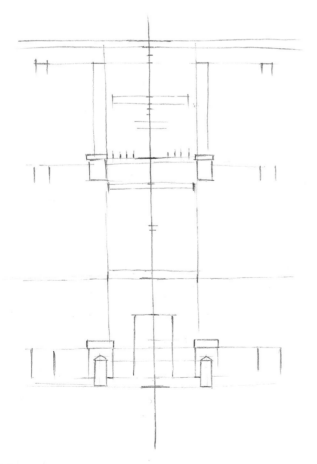

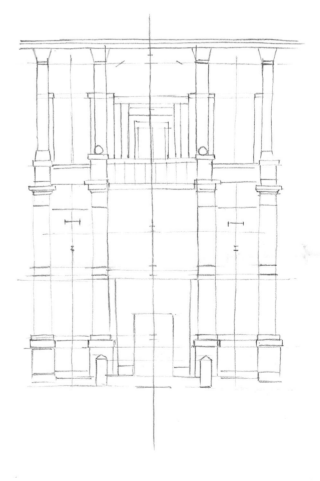

You can check the width of objects by holding the pencil horizontally; incline the pencil to check the angle of slopes.

Verticals and horizontals

To ensure accuracy and correct proportion in your drawing, you can create a grid on which to place all the elements that form your subject.

Once I'd outlined the basic structure of the entrance, I started to add details such as blocks and windows (*below*). These should always be drawn last so as not to distract from the proportions of the subject. My finished drawing (*right*) was done with a 2B pencil on Bockingford paper

Measure above and below, and to either side (respectively) when adding the other verticals and horizontals. Use pencil measuring to achieve the correct proportions.

Start by drawing a faint horizontal line across the middle of your paper at eye level. Then draw a vertical line down its length. These lines will be at the centre of your grid; use them as points of reference for the object you are drawing.

Gradually build up your drawing. First, add the other main verticals and horizontals, such as doorways and windows; then go on to add detail to finish it off.

Using Shapes in Drawing

When you begin drawing, you may be overwhelmed by a building's complexity. You may find that the finished drawing doesn't look right and doesn't seem to 'work'. It is helpful to remember that a building consists of various solid forms that have a spatial relationship to each other. Your powers of observation will improve and drawing will become easier once you can understand how these forms and relationships work together.

Reducing a house to a silhouette will make you ignore superficial detail. The silhouette here (*right*) is really just a large square and two

rectangles, yet compare it with the fully detailed house at the bottom of p. 17! I've drawn some more diagrams to help you understand how to illustrate the detail. Compare each one with the detailed version.

This sketch (*right*) expresses the house in vertical lines and emphasizes the vertical spaces between parts of the house. Eliminating the visual distraction of the horizontal gutter under the eaves makes you more aware of the true depth between the roof ridge and windows

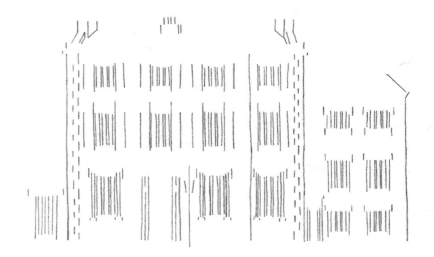

Here, the house has been expressed as a series of horizontal strokes (*right*) to show the horizontal spatial relationships. Notice the width of the gaps between the windows

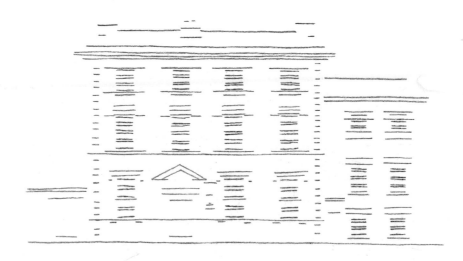

As well as looking at geometric forms, you'll learn a lot about how a building 'works' by reducing it to light and dark areas. You'll see that I've rendered the different shades as either black or white (*left*). I eliminated all lines except the bare minimum needed to hold the shape together

'Dissect' as many different buildings as possible. Try to use shapes such as circles or triangles, as well as squares and rectangles. You can work from life or use photographs. After a while, your eye will become trained and you'll be able to represent a building accurately without dissecting it.

The finished drawing (*below*), complete with shading, was done with a 2B pencil on tracing paper

As you analysed the two-dimensional forms of the house, you can now go on to discover how any building can be broken down into simple, easily drawn, solid geometric forms.

It's a good idea to practise drawing basic forms. The main ones you'll need are cubes, cuboids (box shapes with unequal faces), tubes or cylinders, prisms and pyramids. The section on perspective (pp. 20–25) will help you draw them from different viewpoints. Once you can sketch buildings using the simpler shapes, you may feel ambitious enough to use a half sphere as the basis from which to draw a domed building.

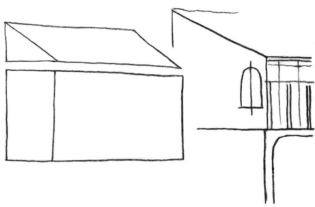

The basic solids you'll need are (*below*) a cylinder, a cuboid, a cuboid seen from a different viewpoint, a cone and a pyramid

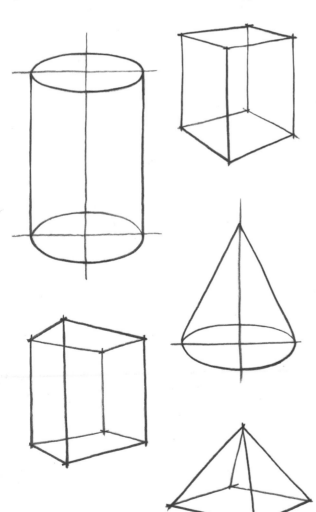

The old houses opposite may look a hopeless confusion of forms, but like any other building, they break down into simple forms (*above*). The wall that supports the main roofs is common to all three houses. It is a single plane to which you can attach all the balconies, which are made up from cuboids and prisms.

I drew these old houses in Enkhuizen, in the Netherlands, with a B pencil on Bristol board. You'll find that even the most complex building or group of buildings can be reduced to basic geometric units

When you feel confident drawing solid shapes, you can use them to create a finished picture of a building. By using one shape as the basis from which to 'build', you can add other geometric shapes until you have the outline of your subject. Then you can add the detail.

Space and Perspective

Space and planes

Representing three-dimensional buildings on a flat, two-dimensional surface (paper) requires an understanding of perspective and space. When looking at objects, those nearer you look larger than those further away. To help you with drawing in perspective, measure the relative sizes of close and distant objects with a pencil.

We can divide the space in which objects lie into three planes: the **far distance** – the furthest plane; the **middle distance** – closer to you; the **foreground** – nearest to you. On paper, you combine these three planes to make your drawing, remembering that objects diminish in size the further they are from you. This view on your paper becomes a fourth plane, the **picture plane,** in which objects near and far appear to be next to each other.

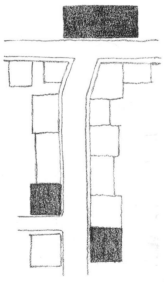

In the diagram (*top*), I have shaded three buildings in the far distance, middle distance and foreground. The same buildings have also been shaded in the plan view of the street above

In the drawing (*left*), you can see the recessional values of space at work, giving depth to the scene

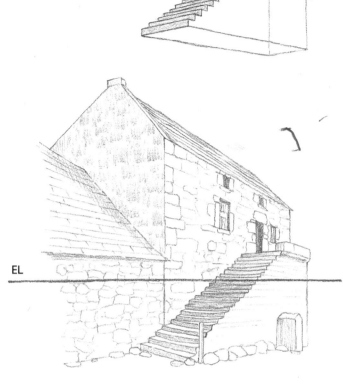

Viewpoint

Your **viewpoint** is the position from which you look at a subject. If you stand below a building you will not be able to see the top of it. If, however, you are level with its top you will see less of its bottom. Therefore, viewpoint is important when selecting a position from which to draw your subject.

Eye-level

Your eye-level is an imaginary horizontal plane running from your eyes for as far as you can see. The horizontal lines of buildings (unless parallel with you) will appear to slope down to a point in the distance, if they are above your eye-level, or slope up to the same point if they are below your eye-level.

As your viewpoint changes, so will objects seen below and above your eye-level.

EL

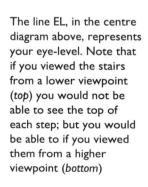

The line EL, in the centre diagram above, represents your eye-level. Note that if you viewed the stairs from a lower viewpoint (*top*) you would not be able to see the top of each step; but you would be able to if you viewed them from a higher viewpoint (*bottom*)

The final drawing was done in B pencil on cartridge paper

The arches and columns, drawn lightly in pencil above, direct the eye to a central vanishing point

One-point perspective

An understanding of perspective lets you draw convincing three-dimensional objects. The sketch above perfectly illustrates **one-point perspective**. The receding horizontals converge to a point on your eye-level. This point is the **vanishing point** (1). The vertical structures are also affected. The further away they are, the smaller they appear. They also seem to get closer together, the spaces between them becoming more narrow, as they recede.

If you move nearer the pillars on the right (2), the horizontal lines of these pillars will converge at much steeper angles than those further away, on the left.

1

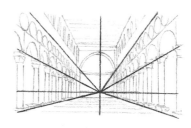

2

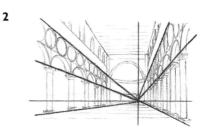

1 Here, you can see how the horizontal receding lines converge to a point on your eye-level, at the centre of your vision, the vanishing point

2 You see less of the pillars on the right, if you move to the right, and more of those on the left. This affects the angle of horizontal convergence

A two-point perspective of the Parthenon in Athens drawn with a 2B pencil on cartridge paper. The main lines of perspective are shown in the simplified diagram (**3**)

Two-point perspective

If you view a building with one of its vertical corners in the centre of your vision, two of its sides will be visible. The horizontal lines on either side of this central vertical line will converge. There will be two vanishing points – one on either side of the central vertical – and they will both be at eye-level. You will be using a **two-point perspective** if you draw a building from this viewpoint.

Moving vanishing points

Vanishing points change as you move around a building. The horizontal lines on the side that you move towards will converge at a shallower angle, and the vanishing point will be further away, than on the other side. For example, if you moved to the left of the central vertical of the Parthenon (*above*), the vanishing point on its left would seem to move further away as the one on the right would seem to move closer (**4**).

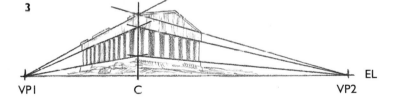

3 This diagram shows two vanishing points, VP1 and VP2, of the Parthenon drawing (*top*). C is the centre of your vision, and EL is your eye-level. Note how the pillars (and the spaces between them) on both sides of C become smaller as they recede

4 As you move around the building to the left, so VP1 will move further away from C and VP2 will move closer. If you were to move so far round that you saw only the left side, the horizontals would be parallel, with no visible vanishing points

I used rectangles drawn in perspective as a guide for the receding windows and gaps between the timbers of these Brittany shops

These simple construction lines show you how to mark off equal horizontal distances along two parallel lines receding towards a vanishing point

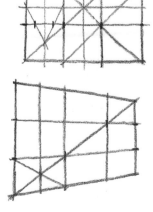

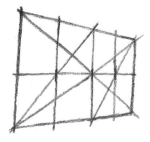

Divisions

Any shape drawn in perspective that is not parallel to the picture plane will be distorted. Luckily, basic geometry shows us how to cope with these distortions.

Diagonals drawn from the corners of a square or rectangle mark the figure's centre where they cross. A vertical and a horizontal line drawn through this centre-point will give the mid-points of the figure's sides. This holds true even on a rectangle drawn in perspective with converging top and bottom sides. This geometric property allows you to draw in perspective a row of windows of equal size.

These ruined arches may look like a nightmare to draw, but once you reduce them to squares seen in perspective, it's really not hard to sketch ellipses inside them to represent half-circles seen in perspective

Circles and ellipses

A circle drawn inside a square just touches the sides of the square at their mid-points. A circle seen in perspective becomes an ellipse, but it will still just touch the inside mid-points of the sides of a square drawn round it in perspective. Use these points of contact on the square as guides for drawing a circle or a half-circle in perspective. The resulting ellipse should look as if it lies in the same plane as the square. Use the pencil measuring method to help get the correct proportions of a square in perspective. You are now ready to begin drawing arched windows and doors, arches, round towers and any other circles in perspective.

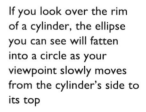

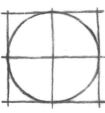

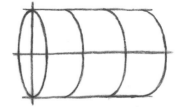

If you look over the rim of a cylinder, the ellipse you can see will fatten into a circle as your viewpoint slowly moves from the cylinder's side to its top

Light and Shade

Light and shade

You can show the three-dimensional form of a subject by using tones and shading to represent shadows cast by light. Strong, direct light – such as a brightly shining sun – will create dark, well-defined shadows. More muted light or light from several sources – such as lamps in a room – will create softer, less black shadows.

There are two ways we refer to shadow. The areas which the light does not reach will be dark – these are **in shadow**. The shadows created by objects as light hits them from one side are **cast shadows**. You might have cast shadows on areas in shadow, requiring you to use different degrees of shading.

The towers below were drawn on cartridge paper with a 2B pencil. Light from the left leaves the main tower's right side in deepest shadow and casts a shadow along the ground to the right. The curved wall is shown as a series of flat surfaces

A great house such as this (*above*) provides excellent practice for applying light and shade. Charcoal on cartridge paper gave enough variety of tone to convey all the different shadow strengths

Use your perspective skills to draw a three-dimensional building. Note the light source and how it casts shadows and highlights on your subject. Make sure when you draw several buildings together that they all have one light source coming from the same direction. Treat all items as one picture, not single buildings.

Receding and protruding shapes

The large drawing at the top consists of many different shapes, some large, some small.

You might be put off drawing something that appears so complex. Yet careful observation of the strengths and tones of the different shadows will help you to draw the building in a way that will clearly show which parts protrude and which parts recede.

I brushed ink wash on to smooth paper to create the strong shadows of bright early morning sun on these Sussex seafront buildings. There are no variations of tone between black and white, but the buildings still have shape and form

Surface Texture

Invented texture

We build texture on paper by describing the tactile qualities of surface textures as patterns of lines, light and shade, using pencils, pens, charcoal, pastels, paints, and so on. When inventing patterns to represent textures, to avoid repetition and to leave something to the imagination, it is a good idea to suggest, for example, just a few bricks in a wall, or a few tiles on a roof (*left*). Thus, drawing a large brick wall will not become a laborious task.

A good way to learn about representing texture is to look at drawings and paintings, in galleries or books, to see what other artists have done. You will notice when doing this that not only do they invent textures to simulate real texture, but they also create texture to convey mood and emotion.

The bold strokes of a 2B pencil on cartridge paper, in this drawing of a group of houses, help to convey strong sunlight, which reflects off the rooftops and creates dark shadow in unlit areas

I carefully drew the shapes and textures of the stonework and tiles of this French villa (*above*) on textured paper with a technical pen. You needn't draw in every single stone or leaf to convey texture – I left large areas here blank

We do not usually notice texture unless we touch or feel it; yet, in real life, there are textures all around us. Texture is therefore very important in drawing to help suggest the surfaces of the objects we wish to draw: the roughness of bricks; the smoothness of glass; the glossy, painted surface of a window frame; or the fluffy texture of clouds.

On paper, we represent the real textures of things by using **invented texture**.

Mood and texture

As well as representing tactile qualities, you can invent abstract simulations of texture to convey sensation and mood. To do this, you exploit the qualities of the paper and tools with which you are working. You can then create bold and strong texture, as in the drawing of the group of houses opposite, or light and open texture, as in the drawing of the French villa. Experimentation is the best way to create abstract texture to portray the emotion you want in your drawings.

Fine detail was not used in the drawing of this castle. Rather, the effect produced by HB pencil on textured paper has been exploited

Sketching

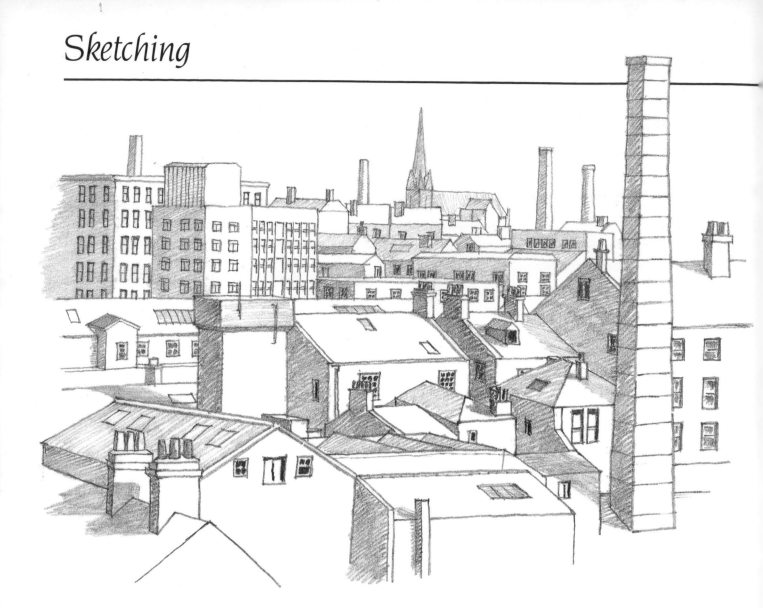

Developing sketching skills

The drawings in this book give an idea of the many different drawing styles. Practise sketching in as many different styles as possible. Much of your skill in drawing will come from developing your ability to interpret the world around you. Nothing improves this skill more than constant sketching from life. Whenever possible, carry a sketchbook with you and use it to record what you see, making notes about tone and colour (see p. 32).

Style and sketching tools

A sketchbook is a visual diary; it is for you alone. Don't worry about mistakes or trying to make each sketch perfect – focus instead on experimenting and practising. Some extremely elegant drawings are made with just simple

This townscape employs perspective, shading and overlapping shapes. It was drawn with a B pencil on tracing paper

black line on white paper. Others suggest light and shadow using a wide variety of tones or textured patterns. The sketch at the top of the opposite page shows a concern for the basic form of the subject. The farmhouse below it shows effective use of textured patterns.

You'll find you prefer using some pens or pencils to others. Some people like the ease and freedom of pencil, while others feel their sketching is improved by the greater discipline needed for technical or dip pens.

This simple HB-pencil sketch on smooth cartridge paper was the basis for a watercolour. I was more concerned with the form of the structures than conveying light and shade or texture, which I intended to create with the paint

I quickly sketched this old farmhouse with a B pencil on cartridge paper to give a rough impression of how the light and shade fell on different parts of the building

Sketching to paint

Two-dimensional images are flat and show only one side of a building. They are useful for practice, but can make beautiful finished drawings in their own right. The sketches of an Amsterdam street (*below*) are working studies for a painting. The artist superimposed another house on the main sketch, raising it to clear the bicycles and street furniture in the first sketch. Extra sketches and notes enable an artist to combine the most attractive details in the final version.

These pen and ink sketches of Amsterdam houses include notes on textures and colour that will be useful when doing a final painting

Seeing shapes and space

In every image, the space around the objects is important. Seeing this space is difficult because our eyes are distracted by objects and details.

It helps to find the basic outline shapes of your subject. To do this, imagine your eyes are a camera that is not focused. You can do this by closing your eyelids until you can only see through a narrow slit. Details become blurred and the image can be seen as a silhouette of simple shapes.

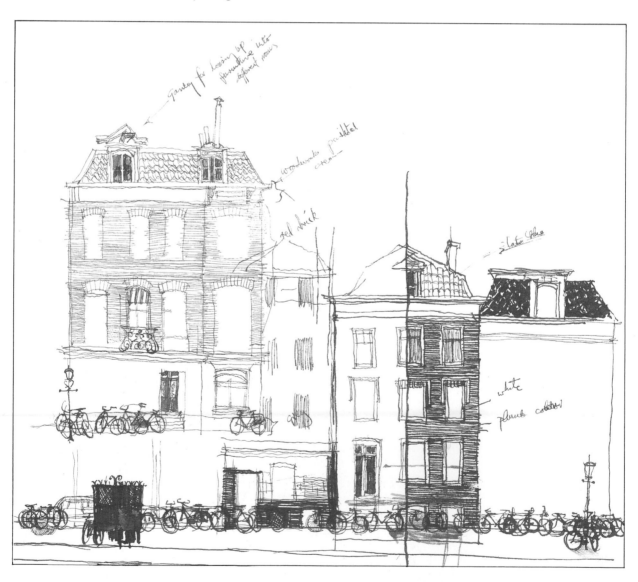

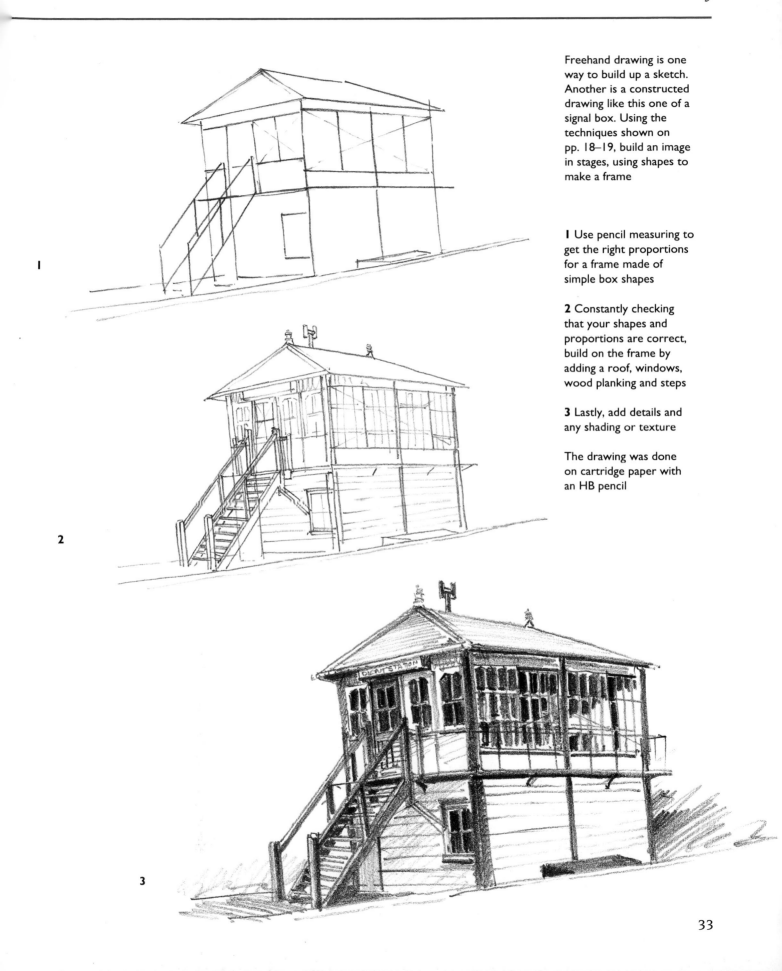

Freehand drawing is one way to build up a sketch. Another is a constructed drawing like this one of a signal box. Using the techniques shown on pp. 18–19, build an image in stages, using shapes to make a frame

1 Use pencil measuring to get the right proportions for a frame made of simple box shapes

2 Constantly checking that your shapes and proportions are correct, build on the frame by adding a roof, windows, wood planking and steps

3 Lastly, add details and any shading or texture

The drawing was done on cartridge paper with an HB pencil

1

2

3

Selecting a Subject

What do you draw?

Good drawing is more than mere technique; it's your feeling that will bring it alive. Anything appealing can make a good subject. A strange building may fascinate you, or you may fall for the wild beauty of a ruined monastery.

When you've developed your skills, you'll want a challenge, like that posed by the cathedral and riverside mill on these pages.

How much detail do you add?

When you've found a subject, decide what is most interesting and where it should appear in your composition. Plan a focus – too much haste can lead to irrelevant, distracting detail or a composition where the focus is confused. There are many ways to change focus – the two drawings here show you one method. The sketch below emphasizes the foreground; the one opposite focuses on the background.

I wanted to focus on the river and the picturesque mill nestling amongst the trees rather than the cathedral towering above and behind them. I drew the area of focus in detail, with strong, dark B-pencil strokes on smooth paper. The bulk of cathedral and its neighbouring buildings are only lightly suggested

Add any architectural detail you need to convey feeling. Remember to make features solid. You need only suggest texture. With a brick wall, for example, draw just a few bricks in empty space – it saves time and the drawing will look less cluttered and much lighter.

Here, I reversed the focus of the picture. Note how the trees and the mill are merely outlined

Framing and Composition

This village on a steep
Mediterranean coast was
drawn in B pencil and fine
felt-tip pen on textured
paper. The pen was used
for the hard edges of the
buildings; pencil shading
added texture

When deciding what to draw, you might feel overwhelmed by the complexity and level of detail in the physical world. Whether you draw a landscape or a building, from life or from a photograph, you must compose your drawing. One large picture or landscape can contain several smaller compositions, as you can see from the drawing opposite and the ones on the right.

To help you decide, try to isolate a particular part of the subject. You can do this by using a frame, either one you make from card or a simple one using your hands. The frame acts like a focus mechanism on a camera, cutting out all extraneous details that you don't want to include in your picture.

Remember when using this framing method that the focus of your composition does not necessarily have to be in the centre. You create the focus of your drawing by using shading to make some areas darker than others: the darker the area, the more the viewer's gaze will be attracted to it.

Card framing

You can make an adjustable frame by cutting two L-shapes from a piece of card (**1**). By putting them together and holding them up to your subject, you can isolate different parts of the subject and see how each appears as a picture on its own. You can also change the size and shape of the frame, which allows you to see how the same subject looks in both a tall and narrow rectangle, and in a square.

You can also make a card frame that is the same size as your drawing surface (**2**).

Hand framing

You can use your hands to frame your subject (**3**). Hold them up in front of you, with the thumbs extended to form the bottom of the frame. Then, as with the card frames, use them to isolate different areas of your subject. Like the first frame (**1**), your hand frame can be adjusted to make different sizes and shapes.

1

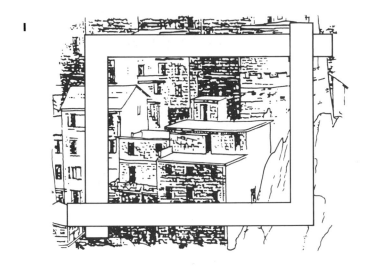

2

3

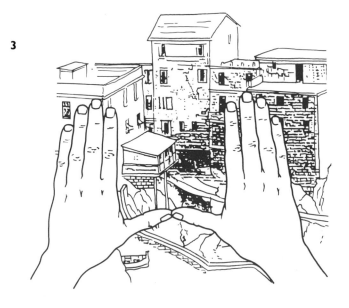

Working Indoors

Drawing indoors imposes fewer constraints than drawing outdoors. You don't have to worry about inconvenient weather conditions, and you can take more time on your drawing. This means you will have more choice of subjects and of media, and it offers the chance to tackle more difficult and detailed drawings.

Drawing in your home

Your own home is a good place to practise drawing interiors. Start by experimenting with foregrounds and backgrounds, aiming to get the correct proportions and relations among objects. Use pencil measuring to test your proportions.

The sketch of furniture and ornaments below was drawn with a B pencil on cartridge paper

You will need to find a comfortable position – either standing at an easel or sitting – that gives you a good, unobstructed view of your subject. Choose a time and position that offer strong natural lighting.

You might practise drawing the same subject from different viewpoints – such as standing, sitting on a chair, and sitting on the ground. Your eye level will change with each position.

Don't feel intimidated by detailed interiors. First get the basic shapes and sense of space. Details can be added later.

Dark but open 2B-pencil strokes on smooth paper convey the airiness of this conservatory (*opposite*)

Thick, 4B-pencil strokes
on tracing paper captured
the contrasts of light in
this medieval barn

Drawing more complex interiors

More complex structures and the interiors of
churches or town halls will stimulate and
challenge you. Animate your drawing and give
it a sense of scale by adding people (see p. 47).

Good light and a comfortable drawing position
are vital – your sketch may take some time. Find
an unobstructed view out of the way of other
people. Use simple, portable equipment: spilled
inks or paints can lead to disaster.

A 2B pencil used on
textured paper conveys
the formality of this
French hotel restaurant

Working Outdoors

Drawing on location

Drawing on location often means working quickly to capture a scene before the light changes or interesting figures move away. Whenever you sketch, you should consider which drawing style best conveys the feel of your subject and how much time you are likely to have for a sketch. Fast, sketchy pencil work may best capture bustling figures in a market, but in a formal study of intricate carving on a cathedral entrance, you can afford the time for a detailed pen and ink study.

Where to sit or stand

Find a spot where you won't attract attention. Concentration is harder outdoors, so try to find a position free of distractions.

Be sure to find a comfortable spot. Combining comfort with the best vantage point can be hard, so try several spots before you settle down.

Tools to take

Take portable equipment that you can easily carry in a shoulder bag. Sketchpads are best, as they provide a hard surface on which to work.

Consider your working conditions. Paints and inks require water and jars, and may not be practical. Start with a range of pencils and pens. Other useful items include clips, tape, tissues and perhaps a sealed container of water for cleaning brushes or creating effects. Look after your tools and don't leave anything behind!

Distance from a subject

The distance between you and your subject is determined as much by your composition as it is by practical concerns, especially if a subject is on private land or in a dangerous spot.

Try to see your entire subject. Even if you draw only part of a building, you'll find you understand it better if you can see all of it.

Position yourself parallel to your subject so that you need only move your eyes — not your entire head — from one side to the other (*above*)

Also, decide whether you want to sit or stand. You could use a lightweight folding chair on level ground. If this is not possible, a comfortable spot on dry ground may provide a good vantage point. If you do a more detailed study, you may prefer to stand and work at an easel

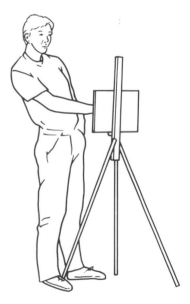

For this church, I used a ball-point pen on smooth paper. Though good for simple sketches, ball-point pen can be messy if shading is overworked

I sketched this French village with a B pencil on cartridge paper. I had no time to make colour notes, so I took some colour snaps to help me with my painting when I got home

Drawing glass

Drawing the glass in windows can be like trying to draw the invisible. To help you to draw glass, begin by familiarizing yourself with the way windows look under different conditions.

Observe as many types of window as you can; in particular, compare those that are near with those that are far away, and those in sunlight with those in shade. Curtains, shutters, interiors behind windows, and even the frames of the windows affect the appearance of glass.

This drawing of a coffee house (*left*), in ball-point pen on Bristol board, illustrates the various ways in which glass can be represented

You can tell when a window is open or closed – a closed one reflects light , as shown below in 2B pencil on smooth paper

Transparency

Glass is transparent, which means that you often don't see it at all, but you know when a window has glass in it and when it doesn't. Although transparent, it is affected by light, shadows and reflections.

The presence of glass in windows can be suggested by using tones. Vary the tones you use in each window pane, trying not to make them all identical. To avoid monotony in your drawings, try not to draw every pane in detail.

The drawing below, in H pencil on smooth paper, shows a lit interior. Glass seems more transparent here than when the interior is dark (*opposite*)

Reflections

Another quality of glass is the way it reflects the world outside. This can be confusing for both the artist and the viewer, as other buildings, trees and even people can appear reflected in the glass of windows. On a tall building, the windows high up may appear lighter than those nearer the ground because the high windows reflect the sky, which is brighter than the buildings and other objects reflected in the lower windows. It often helps to limit the amount of reflected detail you include.

In strong sunlight, you will find that glass reflects the things around it, as I've shown in the drawing below, using ball-point pen on tracing paper

Street Life

You can enliven your drawing by adding street life and street furniture. People, cars, bicycles, lampposts, benches and phone boxes all add excitement and a sense of realism to your scene. Little details add telling atmosphere. A scene in a run-down part of town might include scrawled graffiti, peeling posters and pavement litter.

Street activity and street furniture

Street markets, busy city avenues, even country lanes abound with life and objects unique to that particular environment. The more information you include in your drawing, the more the viewer can sense the location, life and atmosphere of the scene.

In a French street, for example, letter boxes, wastepaper bins, telephone boxes and even the lettering on shops have a distinctive look that will help evoke a French feel to your drawing.

This pen and ink sketch on cartridge paper of Düsseldorf (below) lacks great detail, but a German shop sign and an avenue of trees, which is unusual in Britain, tell us that we are in a foreign country

I jotted down examples of street furniture (above), people and animals (opposite) in a sketchbook. It's an ideal way to collect and store details that can be incorporated in larger drawings or paintings. I often use details I sketched many years ago

Even if I carry nothing else, I always make sure I have a fountain pen and small sketchbook to capture scenes like this (*above*), of a tradesman delivering from a horse-drawn cart

People and animals

People are vital to animate any scene. The presence of people and animals gives a sense of proportion, size and scale, and adds 'local colour', conveying the feel of the culture or customs, and maybe the uniqueness, of the place you have sketched.

Be careful not to clutter your drawing with too much detail. It helps to draw a few figures and other details first, then draw buildings and landscape around them. You can always add more figures later.

47

A square like the one on these pages is busy at most times. To convince, you need people in your drawing. But people interact with their surroundings – they window-shop, they wait at red lights, they admire the view from a park bench, they clean windows and they take snaps. Running or walking figures will add purpose and movement to a scene. Remember, too, that people interact with each other – show couples walking hand-in-hand, parents scolding a naughty child, someone giving directions or children playing.

I used pen and ink to draw this popular American tourist town. I chose cartridge paper to work on because I knew it wouldn't buckle when I added lots of ink. I varied my pen pressure to emphasize different aspects. I used heavy strokes for the statue to convey a sense of its solidity. The movement of the people is suggested by lighter, fluid strokes. Ink takes time to dry, so I carefully dabbed the finished statue with tissue paper to prevent smudging

49

Buildings in Settings

Landscape can give vital clues to a building's locality and place in history. A mountain chalet sketch would mean little if you left out the mountains. A Norman castle drawn without the defensive hill on which it stands would remove it from its historical context and rob your drawing of much of its power.

Seasons and time

Trees can help show the time of year. In spring, buds or immature leaves reveal most of a tree's branches. By summer, mature leaves obscure most of the branches; in autumn, dead leaves litter the ground and branches begin to show again. Bare branches, of course, indicate winter. Shadows are telling clues to the time of day. A low early morning or late afternoon sun casts long shadows, but in the middle of the day an overhead sun casts much shorter shadows.

I drew this French château with felt-tip pen on cartridge paper. The full tree foliage and open flowers suggest that it is summer. The flowers and bricks give visual clues to the wall's height, which in turn helps us to visualize the size of the château

A detailed, high-key drawing of this Mississippi farmstead was made in pen and ink on textured paper. Imagine the building without any of the objects around it. We wouldn't know it was a farm house. We might not even know it was in America without the car and truck parked outside

Size and scale

A building lacks meaning if we don't know its size. Doors and windows on a house show scale because we instinctively relate them to the human figure. But a building like a high-tech factory may provide no easy clues to its size. Add people, cars or any other familiar objects to give scale to these sorts of buildings.

Showing a building's function

There can be little doubt about the role of a church. But function is not always obvious in architecture. For example, if you draw a small country station on a preserved steam railway, you might find the best viewpoint obscures any posters or lettered signs that are clues to its function as a station. If you don't include any surrounding railway detail, it may be difficult to recognize what your drawing represents. But the addition of a steam locomotive with smoke drifting from its chimney would immediately tell us that this is a railway station. A few coaches in a siding, a porter in old-fashioned uniform and some signals would be finishing touches for a drawing full of atmosphere.

This felt-tip pen on cartridge paper sketch of a church perched on a hill shows the sort of old town we would all like to visit. Yet without the buildings, the sketch would simply show an ordinary church to which few people would give a second thought

On the previous pages you saw how surroundings and associated detail convey information and lend atmosphere to an individual building. Similar principles apply when you're drawing a townscape, when, by definition, you want to capture some of the flavour of a town and not just a single building set in isolation.

A mining town set in a steep-sided valley may yield interesting Victorian terraced houses. If you concentrate on just a few houses and ignore the rest of the town, you'll lose the sense of row upon row of houses seeming to tumble down the valley sides. The distant parts of your drawing don't need to be drawn in detail – a few simple pencil strokes to show receding roof tops and chimneys can do the trick.

A sense of history

In a medieval town you usually find that public buildings, like the church or corn exchange, are in prominent positions. A cathedral might sit on a high spot in the town, so that it can be seen from a great distance. A guildhall, for instance, was an important meeting place for the dignitaries of the town, so its builders would often place it in an open square with room for people and horses to gather.

It would be an idea to try to see the guildhall and its square as a whole – taking such buildings out of context deprives them of historical meaning and reduces the visual impact their settings bestow. A modern market held in an old square would make an interesting contrast of old and new.

Marketplace activity

People and street clutter convey the atmosphere of a busy town. Nowhere is this more obvious than in a market. For example, many European towns retain their old 19th-century fruit and vegetable markets, which are often jewels of architectural detail. You could concentrate solely on the elaborate wrought-iron pillars supporting spacious curved glass roofs. But the busy chaos of a market – stalls piled high with crates of leeks, lorry drivers unloading bulging onion nets, porters wheeling trollies laden with potato sacks, dealers haggling over apples, and the trampled debris of squashed fruit, wrappers and broken crates – is what makes a market a living part of a town or city.

In summer, this German cathedral square teems with tourists. But I wanted my pen and ink study to show it on a winter afternoon. Bare trees lend a chilly feeling. Empty market stalls and a few solitary figures add an almost melancholy touch. Had I not included benches, trees and cobblestones to suggest a public square, the building could easily have been in the country

Creating a setting

Using your memories of various places, weather conditions, light effects and atmospheres, you can begin to create your own settings in your drawings. You may have a wonderful drawing of a building on its own that lacks life and atmosphere, to which you can add people and objects to enhance its surroundings.

Look in your sketchbooks for old sketches of artefacts and scenes that may help, or go out and sketch objects you would like to add to your drawing. You can even look in books, magazines or newspapers for helpful images or ask your friends or family to pose briefly for you to catch the stance of a figure you want to introduce to your drawing.

Remember to think about space, viewpoint and perspective when you add people or objects.

People drawn some distance apart from each other, and in perspective, will differ in size. Those in the far distance will be smallest while those in the foreground will be largest. Their feet, in the picture plane, will be on different levels: the further away the subjects are, the higher their feet will be. But their heads will appear to be on one broad level – your eye-level.

Once you have your composition, work out where you want your light source to come from and think about atmosphere: will it be a sunny summer day, or a dreary, wet and windy winter morning?

From the beach house sketches in my sketch-book (*below*) and sketches I made from books and magazines of boats (*right*), I created a beach setting (*opposite*). I changed the size of the boats to give the drawing depth. The final drawing was done in HB pencil on watercolour paper

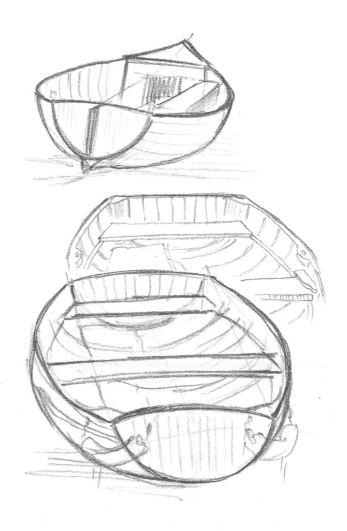

Working from Photographs

Photographs offer a range of exciting subjects not available for drawing from observation, and they are a good way to increase your confidence.

Drawing from photographs enables you to work indoors, take more time and use a wider range of tools than if you were drawing on location.

You will need to do some adapting when drawing from photographs. Simply tracing or copying will not produce the best results or provide the opportunity for experimenting.

Adapting the **contrast** can produce a stronger image. A photograph is made up of a range of tones; reproducing it using only black and white will emphasize some parts of the image more than others, creating a strong impression.

Recomposing is another type of adaptation. For instance, you may wish to change the positions of buildings, walls, windows, doors or trees, or leave some of them out, to enhance your composition.

It is a good idea to take more than one photograph of a subject if you can. Photograph it from different angles and distances in order to capture a greater variety of aspects. This will help when you begin to draw detail.

In the photograph (*left*), the tower in Sintra, Portugal, is captured in its setting of stone walls, battlements, and creeping foliage. However, it is very hard to distinguish the detail at the top of the tower. A second photograph (*above*) helps to show this detail. In the 2B drawing opposite, note how I changed the composition and represented the texture of different surfaces

Looking After Your Drawings

Drawings in certain media risk increasing damage the more they are handled. So, once your drawing is finished, it should be cared for properly.

Fixing

Drawings in pencil, pastel, charcoal, wax, conté crayon and chalk must be fixed to prevent smudging when handled. Spray fixatives are available, or you can use a diffuser to blow the fixative solution gently on to your artwork. The latter is safer for you and the environment.

To apply fixative evenly, stand half a metre away from your drawing. Allow it to dry before handling.

Storing

If you are not going to frame your drawing immediately, prepare to store it carefully in a flat, dry place. Make sure fixative or any wet media used is dry, then place the drawing flat, putting sheets of clean tissue paper between it and other stored drawings.

I applied fixative to this 2B-pencil drawing of Hastings (the old quarter) on smooth paper to keep the soft pencil from smudging

This Greek Byzantine monastery in Mistra was drawn with B and 2B pencils on textured paper. Fixative was applied so that the sharpness of the pencil lines would not be lost through handling

Using Your Drawings

Cards

You can derive much pleasure and pride from seeing your artwork reproduced on cards and stationery. Select your work carefully for printing; simple, clean drawings reproduce well. Colour is more expensive to print, so consider this when selecting. Also, keep in mind that the printed result will not exactly match your original. With experience, you will learn how to achieve certain effects for printed work and you will be better able to predict final results.

Holiday and birthday cards are made more special with the personal touch your artwork adds. You might want to have a sketch of your house, covered in snow, featured on a Christmas card.

You can use transfer letters such as Letraset (*top*), draw your own lettering (*right*), or get a printer to do typesetting for you (*below*)

You can use your drawings in a variety of ways: on Christmas cards, postcards, greetings cards and so on. Not only will this add a personal touch, but it might save you money, too

Party invitations and
change-of-address cards
will be all the more
memorable decorated
with your own artwork

*Tim will be 30 on Saturday March 2nd.
You are invited to celebrate his birthday
at a party beginning at 8pm at
The Pedlinge Hotel, Barne*

Kate & John
have moved to:

'The Retreat'
Lower Road
Postcombe
Oxfordshire
OX9 7DU

Tel: 0844 31672

Invitations to special events are also made
more exciting and memorable when enhanced
with your own artwork. Be sure to include
all the necessary information in a clear and
straightforward way. If you live in the country
or somewhere hard to find, you could include a
sketch map of how to reach your home, showing
little drawings of landmarks to look out for on
the way. For a change-of-address card, consider
drawing pictures of both your old home or town
and your new home or town.

Bookmarks decorated
with buildings and printed
on stiff, coloured card will
make attractive little
presents that will give
friends and relatives a

permanent reminder of
you. If you run a business,
you could include the
name of your company to
remind your clients of
what you can offer

Stationery

You can design your own letterhead by having one of your drawings printed on standard stationery paper. You could also design the lettering that goes underneath it. This could be used for business or personal correspondence, and it would be sure to convey something about you to the recipient.

Stationery headed with a drawing of your home gives your personal correspondence a unique and delightful touch. Use artwork of your own company premises to add a touch of class to your business letters

Lee Eccleston
Duckets Cottage
Hamperden End
Debden Green
Essex CM21 3BL

Tel: 0484 67312

BISHOPS MILL • RIVINGTON LANE • HONITON • DEVON • EX17 3BG
TEL: 0404 21639

This exhibition poster could be photocopied on coloured paper. If you require many posters, printing need not be expensive. To make a poster more lively, you could print the artwork in a different colour from the type

Artwork can be used to enliven magazine articles (*below*). It should be appropriate, though, for the tone of the topic discussed. For example, it would be inappropriate to illustrate an academic piece on Saxon churches with a cartoon!

JAMES DALLAS

An Exhibition
of his Work at

The Castle Museum
Hythe

January 20 – 29, 1993
Open Daily: 10am – 8pm. Admission Free

Posters and magazines

Lively posters can grab attention. Whether it advertises a product or an event, a poster works best with bold, large images. Your drawing could also be used to illustrate a book or magazine article. Original artwork is an effective way to catch a reader's attention and keep it.